BACKPACKING
TO THE MOON

BACKPACKING TO THE MOON

How Two Backpackers Built a Vacation-Rental
Empire and Then Became the Largest Sustainability
Real Estate Developer in Tulum, Mexico

MARC LEVY & NICO WILMES

JONES MEDIA PUBLISHING

Disclaimer:

The author strives to be as accurate and complete as possible in the creation of this book, notwithstanding the fact that the author does not warrant or represent at any time that the contents within are accurate due to the rapidly changing nature of the Internet.

While all attempts have been made to verify information provided in this publication, the Author and the Publisher assume no responsibility and are not liable for errors, omissions, or contrary interpretation of the subject matter herein. The Author and Publisher hereby disclaim any liability, loss or damage incurred as a result of the application and utilization, whether directly or indirectly, of any information, suggestion, advice, or procedure in this book. Any perceived slights of specific persons, peoples, or organizations are unintentional.

In practical advice books, like anything else in life, there are no guarantees of income made. Readers are cautioned to rely on their own judgment about their individual circumstances to act accordingly. Readers are responsible for their own actions, choices, and results. This book is not intended for use as a source of legal, business, accounting or financial advice. All readers are advised to seek the services of competent professionals in legal, business, accounting, and finance field.

Printed in the United States of America

Jones Media Publishing
www.JonesMediaPublishing.com

ISBN: 978-1-948382-00-7 paperback
JMP2020.2

To every entrepreneur with a dream and a vision that will put you on the moon. Your backpack may seem too full, your ambition too great, but with every step upwards the air gets lighter. If we can do it, you can too.

Contents

INTRODUCTION

Two backpackers, Nico and I, decided to hustle, to research, to work hard . . . It was clear: we shared that vision to never give up! We built a house to rent on Airbnb. We provided the best service and put in great effort to make the best accommodation and experience for each guest. After a year of consistency and perseverance, we were able to harvest our hard work and reinvested on building more and more accommodation houses and buildings. It's said that "you harvest what you plant." We later created Los Amigos Tulum, one of the fastest growing companies in the world! From 2 to 350 employees in less than 3 years.

Los Amigos set the most impeccable standards in accommodation, experiences, and real estate in Tulum, Mexico, in terms of quality, dedication, sustainability, and vision. Lots of companies try to replicate its business model, and that is something that Nico and I are fine with—we even like it, because that means we did it! We did a great job! That other companies try to be like us is a grand achievement—a positive for the company as well as for the world, because companies also want to replicate its sustainable practices.

Los Amigos Tulum pioneered the largest solar power system in Tulum, the first wind turbine technology to Latin America from the UK, and a movie theater in the jungle. It built its most popular and breathtaking amenity, the Los Amigos Beach Club. And Nico and I broke a couple world records along the way: driving a Tesla cross-country through Mexico and building the first 360-degree rooftop pool in the world. We're always envisioning growth, envisioning the next step—we go forward, always!

Our vision, once confined to Tulum, extends far beyond Mexico to global markets not yet developed.

If we did it, you can do it too! Now join us on a journey through our experiences, with tips to achieve success.

1

<u>HUMBLE BEGINNINGS</u>

The greatest wealth is to live content with little.

—Plato

I was out of the job when I decided to travel to Central America. It was 2010 and after a tough time in the US economy; I worked in the construction industry and, therefore, got laid off. I had done a lot of traveling in the United States and abroad, but this time I wanted to travel with a purpose!

As an American traveling abroad, you discover that most people in other countries speak at least two languages, yet the average American speaks only English. I liked Spanish in high school and practiced speaking it in my various jobs with coworkers in restaurants, but, of course, just exchanged familiar

Spanish words and phrases. I really wished to learn conversational Spanish, and so I made it my goal to one day live in a Spanish-speaking country to immerse myself in the language.

I started to look online for schools that taught Spanish in Central America. There were many great schools with fees as low as $100 per week. And so, I decided on Antigua, Guatemala, to learn Spanish for a few weeks, then planned to travel by bus through Central America. During this time, I checked into the hostel where I met Nico.

Nico was working at his packaging company in Kassel, Germany. After several years of working like a dog, he trusted his employees to operate the company without him, and from there he set off to travel. Nico was a big-time traveler who had already gone around most of the world. He invested in solar panels in Germany and realized from his travels in Mexico that the solar panel business was very underutilized. He decided he wanted to live in Mexico, but first he needed to learn the language better. He also investigated the same information as me about Antigua, Guatemala, and decided to first take formal classes there. Initially, Nico stayed in a different hostel but had a bad experience there, so he moved to the hostel where, that very day, I had also checked in.

So, fate put us together in the same country, city, and now hostel! And without even knowing it, we both had the same mission and tentative plan.

We initially connected through similar interests in health and fitness (well actually, we initially connected in the hostel bathroom brushing our teeth). We started talking about the gym, and then discovered that we both came to Central America to study Spanish. While everybody else in the hostel partied, we studied Spanish and absorbed the Guatemalan culture (OK, let's be honest, we partied as well for at least the first week). And so, from there we got stuck together. After a few days, and few too many tequilas, we decided to rent an apartment together so we could continue studying. We learned more about each other, and after four weeks in Guatemala, we discovered that we had the same vision to travel around Central America, with no final destination in mind.

Through a common vision, we became travel buddies. Nico always joked, "You just point to a spot on the map, and I look through the guidebooks, do the research, and handle all the planning and scheduling." Little did we know that we'd soon engage in business together and that our different styles would make for a great partnership.

We traveled through Central America together, speaking Spanish with each other and with the locals, for about four months. We went on the traditional Central America tour, heading south through Guatemala, Honduras, El Salvador, Nicaragua, Costa Rica, and Panama. Then we flew to one final city, Medellín, Colombia, because we wished to experience more of the immersive lifestyle; we stayed for one month and lived like locals as we were tired of all the traveling and wanted to speak more Spanish.

However, after Medellín I had to go back home: I was out of money and had to look for a job. Nico moved to a city called San Luis Potosí in central Mexico to live full-time and to further investigate the solar business. Although we split ways in April 2011, we kept in contact mainly via Skype, Nico in Mexico and I in the United States.

We both had an undefined passion and vision for living and working—or doing anything—in Latin

America, but we didn't know how to make it happen. Later that year, while Nico was in Mexico, he told me that there are a lot of construction and land opportunities in Tulum, Mexico, and the Caribbean. And since I'm a construction engineer, Nico discussed with me about partnering in a business venture together. I subrented my apartment where I was living in Arizona, and I earned double of what my rent was. This was the first time I learned about Airbnb. With this money I agreed to meet Nico in Tulum for a few months, study Spanish, and continue online job searching, meanwhile making cool videos with Nico (which is one of his hobbies), and looking at business opportunities— although the latter was the least expected for me at the time. Meanwhile, Nico was overseeing his packaging company in Germany and researching land opportunities, starting a solar business, and the requirements for visas and forming a business in Mexico. I think he took the business part of it more serious than me at this point.

We ended up first living in Playa del Carmen, as Tulum was still very quiet and we decided to live in a place with a bit more action. I taught English classes, which also helped me to learn Spanish, making $3 an hour. Then started doing professional translations on several different projects, such as operating manuals for electronics, architecture/construction documents, and tourism and marketing documents; also, I dared to work as a translator in meetings and events, such as a meeting with two large tour companies (one Russian and the other Mexican) and even a wedding with a Mexican bride and American groom. These gigs were quite difficult and risky at the time because of my intermediate Spanish ability, but the only way to really learn a language is to forget about being embarrassed and just do it.

Also, at the same time, we were looking at several different business options, such as a rental car business, solar energy, and buying land and building—the last being our main focus.

In April 2012 we started a company together even though we didn't know what we were going to do at the time. At the notary—in Mexico this is a lawyer that opens businesses and does other transactions as well—they offered us a name of a company that was already approved but never used. So instead of going through the process of selecting a name, we used the preapproved name, Amigos de la Riviera Maya—coincidentally, we had no idea that we'd eventually name the business Los Amigos. We obtained our first temporary visa, which was quite a time-consuming process, and went about fulfilling the requirements for doing business in Mexico. We always describe the visa process, or doing other government processes in Mexico, as therapy because you have to really learn to be patient. We were still considering different options, with real estate as our main focus, but we were always open to altering, diversifying, and expanding on our initial business model. We even investigated starting a rental car company with old exotic cars since we already had a 1978 Volkswagen (Safari it's called in Mexico).

So that is how the universe worked its magic, and our partnership began! We started with a vision and a love for the Latin culture, language, and people, and then we immersed ourselves in our shared passion until we came up with our business plan.

* * *

TIPS

- Follow your instincts.

- Love what you do.

- Have an idea or a vision of what you want.

- Take the first step!

2

THE PERFECT PLOT OF LAND TO BUILD A COMPANY ON

The path to success is to take massive,
determined action.

—**Tony Robbins**

When we both arrived in Tulum, Mexico, we had a plan that we'd each contribute around $25,000 to spend on a project and to kickstart our business. That was basically all the money I had laying around, including my savings from my construction job in Arizona, 401(k) fund, and a few stocks. The main idea was to buy a piece of land and either build on it or remodel an already existing house.

In the beginning, Nico was running a packaging business in Germany, so he easily met the agreed upon $25,000 contribution with his savings. He had some capital available to him to invest, and he had a business manager still running his business back in Germany. Since we were both in Mexico now, we started looking for land in our local area first, land near Tulum, Playa del Carmen, and the Riviera Maya, although our main focus and goal was always Tulum. The budget was approximately $25,000–$30,000 for land.

Before our first project, we spent months going around the region, investigating lands and looking at all the different options. We were 100 percent hustlers: we were researching each area, each opportunity, nothing stopped us! We met with several real estate companies and agents, and we conducted thorough research. The main goal was to really understand what we were going to do. We had maps in our house with pins and prices on everything: we were just focusing on purchasing land at this point. It's important for anybody who wants to get into a new project, especially in a new country, to make a clearly defined goal and hit it from every angle. You really must get your hands dirty and understand every aspect of a deal before you can make a business decision—for example, whether to purchase land in this or that location.

We researched for several months, and on the sixth month, we finally started making offers. We got rejected several times before we finally bought our first piece of land (within budget!), which cost $30,000. Everybody said it's impossible to find land for that cheap in the locations we were looking, but we knew that we could find it; that's why we looked around so much and researched so heavily. By the time we made our purchase, we knew more about the lands that were available in the area than the actual real estate agents. This price we bought the land for is now impossible in the area: the same land that cost $30,000 in July 2012, now would cost around $100,000. (The main reason the land prices have risen so drastic is for the craze that we caused in the area; the craze this book is about.)

The land we found was in Tulum, where we originally wished to build. The land had an ugly, old property on it. We initially thought we'd just keep the property since we didn't have much additional money to spend; we only wanted to put a few thousand dollars into it and make a hostel or something similar for travelers. After purchasing the land, not much remained in our budget, so we originally thought to just make some minor renovations on the building and run a hostel to generate income. However, we decided against renovating the current property and aimed to build a new house on a small budget. Our original plan was to invest $50,000 in total, so we'd be left with about $20,000 to spend after the land. We knew that building something for that amount was basically impossible, so we told the architects that our budget was around $30,000–$40,000: we still needed to figure out how to raise the funds to build the project.

Next, we began meeting with and interviewing different architects to design the house. In this region, most of the architects are also the contractors, but in the US the two belong to distinct roles. As we interviewed for an architect to design the house, the architect often offered to build it as well as to manage the entire construction process— it's a one-man show for everything down here. But, if you decided against the dual service, the architect would charge you only a little less if you opted out the management portion of the project. Although I had experience in managing construction projects, we decided that it would be for the best to have the architect do everything (design, build, and manage the project) since we were in a foreign country.

When we finally found an architect-contractor who shared our vision, the lowest budget we could get to was approximately $50,000 to build a house on the plot of land. After much research and many meetings between us and our architect, we had to decide if the property would be flashy and modern or quaint and calming. We chose quaint and calming—admittedly, the building cost played the deciding role. The house design was just two stories, with a communal downstairs and separate entrances into the two bedrooms upstairs—we still advertised the house as "luxury" and aspired to put in a pool later on. In our minds, even if we failed, we'd still have a nice house we could use with our families.

The original budget was actually about $62,000, but we took out amenities like a nice perimeter wall and the pool to keep the budget as low as possible. At that point, we didn't have the necessary funds to build the house, but when we saw the architect's plans and potential for this house, what we could envision excited us. We quickly began looking at many different options to raise more capital to fit this new budget. We were extremely nervous about going beyond our budget, but we both decided this was a worthwhile risk and investment.

I sold a car that I had back home in Arizona, used all the credit cards I could, and received a $10,000 loan from my parents. Luckily, I also had invested about $2,000 on 50 shares of Apple stock when it was $40/share in 2005, which I also sold to meet my contribution. (As it happens, in 2014 the stock split 7:1, and my shares would now be worth about $130,000. But, without selling this stock, the company's initial success wouldn't have happened.) By the time we needed to come up with the additional money needed to build the first house, I still couldn't meet my contribution completely, but Nico made up the difference, trusting that I would pay him back once the company became profitable. We had a tremendous level of trust with each other from the beginning, and both of us were sure this land and house was a sound investment that we could profit from and build the company on.

* * *

Tips

- Trust is the most important thing in a partnership.

- Make it happen.

- If you feel it, and you want it, go for it.

- When you put in all your passion and effort, everything will pay off.

- Do as much research and due diligence as possible before starting a new investment.

3

Our First Vacation Rental

Do what you can, with what you have, where you are.

—**Theodore Roosevelt**

Construction on our first property began in October 2012, and we developed a plan and a schedule to finish the property within ten weeks (Did you say ten weeks?!). That may sound fast, but our contractor told us it was possible, and we wanted to have the house ready to rent by the Christmas season, the busiest tourist time in Tulum. As we have learned throughout the years, it's possible to build much faster in Mexico than in other, more developed parts of the world, such as Germany and the United States. While the house was under construction, we posted the property on Airbnb with just a few SketchUp drawings, and before construction was finished, the house was fully booked—we had renters before construction was even completed. At this point, we started realizing the power of Airbnb and the excitement of Tulum.

It's also common for architects to name the project their designing. If the client doesn't have a specific name, then the architect will create an internal name during the project phase at least. Our architect named our project *Casa Los Amigos* (The Friends House). They made it simple as we were two friends (*amigos*) and we were building a simple house (*casa*). And as the project went along, we all called it *Casa Los Amigos* (The Friends House), and that name grew on us, so we ended up using the name on the commercial side for managing the house as well.

We told the architect that renters were already booked a few days before the projected completion date in order to put more pressure on him and, therefore, we needed all the construction completed on time. To provide the vacation experience we wanted, there was no way we could have construction still happening when guests arrived. We needed everything completed on time. Believe it or not, the house was in fact built and completed within ten weeks as planned, and our first guests arrived December 21, 2012. This was the launch of our first Airbnb—the beginning of our success. Our dream came true: it was this indescribable, amazing feeling of achievement!

After seeing the completed house, we thought we'd stay in the house for a portion of the year to experience the amazing house that we built in paradise! At the same time, we also wanted to maintain the rental income as high as possible. If we didn't have renters for a couple of rooms over a couple of nights, we'd go into the center of Tulum at the bus station with an iPad and talk to random people on the streets—tourists, backpackers, travelers—and show the house. Yes, most people thought we were crazy, but we'd always find somebody that believed us. We didn't only list the property on Airbnb and hope for the best; we hustled and constantly worked to spread the word about this property. In the end, we realized we wouldn't be staying there much since the house was rented so often.

Many people didn't believe us about this property, as we'd occasionally drop the rent to around $30 a night so that we could have a renter and the income for the evening. For the first year, we had a 98 percent occupancy rate. (Can you believe it? Who has a 98 percent occupancy rate in a vacation rental or hotel? I think that's impossible, but we achieved it!) From the beginning, we could see we had something special here, with the house and the business; this is when we really saw the power, success, and potential in Tulum.

In total we invested about $100,000 for the land and construction of our first vacation rental house, which to this day is one of our most popular rentals on our Airbnb profile: Marc & Nico.

At the end of the first year operating the rental on Airbnb, we came to realize the overall potential of this property. The rental income the first year was marginal, but small initial returns are expected when starting a new business. I was able to pay back most of the debt that I incurred in order to complete the project. It became obvious to both of us that we had just one house and that operating as a full-time Airbnb host for a living would require building or acquiring more properties.

* * *

Tips

- Opportunities don't knock on your door, so go out, hustle, and make it happen.

- Your initial idea or vision will start making more sense day by day.

- Make your goal 100 percent occupancy; if not, you're not working hard enough.

4

LOOKING FOR AVENUES TO EXPAND

You miss 100 percent of the shots you never take.

—**Wayne Gretzky**

We began aggressively looking for avenues to expand our business. We knew Tulum was an untapped area with unique potential. But, in our current state at the time, in the beginning of 2013, we didn't have the available funds. We just began our vacation rental business, and we were new to the Airbnb platform. We lacked the readily available capital needed to seize a good piece of land when it came on the market. I was just trying to finish paying back my original debt ASAP and living a rather humble life. At this point we had confidence that the rental business was going to keep getting better and better. After about 1 more year of renting, Nico bought another piece of land nearby. This land was a bit shady when he first bought it as the title wasn't clear. Nico has always been a bit crazier than me on making deals. He bought it without me there as he knew I would probably be against it. It costed also around $30,000. Again, he purchased the land trusting that I would also find my way to pay half. At this point we thought the deal was risky and crazy, but nothing compared to some other deals we did later as we continued to expand.

Once we owned the land, we ran into a familiar issue: we needed to raise funds to build the next project. With the success of Casa Los Amigos, we had a lot of confidence in our vision and ability to raise money.

Small wins over time will build confidence; early on it's just a matter of finding out what works and what doesn't. That was true for us. The goal for our next project was, again, to finish for the Christmas season in 2014, the busiest travel season for Tulum. While researching the options and types of houses, a friend of Nico's mentioned the idea of building smaller apartments. We agreed and envisioned something spectacular, but this plot of land was fairly small. After a few discussions about the possible options, we thought of a rooftop pool. At this time no one ever imagined a rooftop pool in Tulum. Tulum was always a sleepy little Mayan village with an incredible beach and rustic homes and shacks; luxury and rooftop pools wasn't a thing. We knew a pool on the roof was so distinctive and unique, it increased our confidence and excitement about this new property. From this project and all the projects to this day, we always look to put wow elements in each of them!

When we decided to build an apartment building, it made sense to have smaller units; this method of short-term vacation rental was more like a hotel room than a traditional apartment unit. The building's design included seven units on three levels. We directed the architect to design the building the maximum height allowable, which for this plot of land is 12 meters high (about 40 feet).

To build this incredible property, we needed about $300,000, which was well beyond what we had combined. This still sounded affordable because something like this in the US would cost well over $1,000,000. In our respective countries, we had spread the word in our circles and on social media about our real estate success in Tulum, Mexico.

We worked with a lawyer to create a basic private lending contract, which allowed friends and family to supply a short-term loan to help us raise capital. The contract costed about $500, which was a lot at the time, and we didn't know if it would work, but decided it was worth the risk.

Like the first project, Nico raised the necessary funds through his own savings and a business loan back in Germany. I compiled a list of friends and acquaintances who knew our business model and who had indicated interest in investing in Tulum. After going through my list and talking to everyone, I later short-listed all the serious ones. I convinced enough people to believe in the project and the business and to invest. Ultimately, the investors and friends believed in us! Through the private lending contract, I was able to fund about $150,000 from just a few friends and investors. The investors agreed to a 10 percent annual return on their investment, plus equity based on their percentage of the investment on the project (not bad, right?!). Each investor had a separately negotiated, slightly different deal. Over the years, each investor was paid back in full with a fair return on their original investment, or investors were given the option to apply their investment towards a new property of ours (already constructed or a future project). When doing the original contracts, we didn't know we'd be developing on a larger scale, so the investment payback plan was quite vague and unclear.

When the money from investors began coming in, we started the project immediately in July 2014. We were told the project would take 5–6 months, which again sounded quick, but we were getting more used to the building speed in Mexico. This would get the project finished in time for Christmas. The property would have an amazing view; the location is unique and exclusive, secluded in surrounding jungle. This private property was one of the first developments in the area, an area of untapped and unbelievable potential.

The building was about 4,500 square feet in total, with an incredible rooftop pool. Since the land was only 3,000 square feet and the building size could only be 3 levels, and considering the setbacks from the boundary lines, this left a pretty compact space. There were 7 units in total, and 1 unit was originally designated for our reception office, storage, and laundry area; we designed this room so that we could later convert it to another hotel room in the future. The building structure was designed to have units of different size. The largest unit was on the top floor; it was 1,400 square feet and could even be divided into two units for guests if wanted. The 1-bedroom suites in the middle were 750 square feet each. There were 4 small studio units on the bottom floor, each 350 square feet (one being our multiuse office area). Little did we know these studio units were going to be such a hit!

We wanted to be hands-on with this property, and not worry about living in luxury, so we lived quite modestly throughout the project. We finished the project on time, rooftop pool and all, on December 20, 2014, to welcome our first guests, and we had had the apartments fully rented through Airbnb before construction was completed. Building properties with small hotel-type units was unheard of in Tulum and in most parts of the world. Over time, this building design has become increasingly common as other property developers and boutique hotels watched our growth and success over the years. This rental type is now the most common building design in Tulum and the Riviera Maya.

That project was a huge success, which gave us and our investors a great return on investment. Because of the time of year we introduced this property—in the winter—the rental income was incredibly high. We rented the units for $300–$700 per night during Christmas and New Year's. The property was named Condos Los Amigos: we went with the same architect as Casa Los Amigos and named the property just like the first. From there this helped us define our business name on a commercial level; each of our successive properties followed the Los Amigos branding, which promised luxury and aesthetics. We provided our guests with whatever they could imagine. We noticed that our guests liked the amenities and design of the rooftop pool property, and that they didn't mind paying premium rates for simple yet appreciative treatment. With this property, we knew we had something special. This was the tipping point of our journey in the vacation rental business, and we fully committed to the vision defined by this property. We took greater risks to go all in in Tulum, confident the area would explode. If it didn't, we'd develop it into a boomtown, because we absolutely knew there was potential here.

THE ACCELERATION OF OUR BUSINESS

When it came time for the next property, we needed more investors. We advertised the construction for a similar condo hotel project. Along with the same investors and some new additions, we were able to fund the next big project. We used the same contract with investors (the price of the contract didn't seem so expensive anymore). We began construction on the third property in May 2015, and our goal was to finish it in time for the high season at the end of the year. The project actually finished in October 2015, which gave us time to furnish and be extra prepared for the busy season. This project was a similar style condo building, but with only 5 units. The goal of this building was to operate it without a reception and more of a self check-in building. Also, we designed a rooftop pool even more incredible than the first since it has an infinity edge into the sunset. We call it Sky Condos, or, internally, Condos Los Amigos 3.

At this point, the money was beginning to accumulate. We started buying more land, building units with our cashflow, no longer relying on investors. With our business growth, we were able to increase the number of rentals we owned through the profits of our previous investments. Over the next 2 years we built 4 more projects in different locations, 19 units on 7 different pieces of land. When we refer to units, it can be a 350-square-foot studio or 2,500-square-foot private home. By the end of 2016 as we had everything operating, our revenue was already close to $1 million annually!

It's incredible to think back on the progression of investment properties and how they became more and more dynamic. Our first house was completed in December 2012. The first condo hotel with 7 units was completed in December 2014. The second condo hotel, which has 5 units, was completed in October 2015. During this time, we also built a house with 2 separate residences and a pool between the 2 living spaces called Oasis Los Amigos. That property created additional cashflow on one plot of land. Also, in 2015, we discovered the land beside Condos Los Amigos was for sale, and had to buy it, although we didn't yet know what to build on it, and we didn't have the capital at the time. Later in the summer of 2016, we built on this land with 3 more units, plus an official reception area, and an official storage/laundry room, and a Flintstones-style gym area in the jungle. We originally intended to live in two of these units, but as the rents were so high at the time and our condos were so occupied and sought after, we elected to sleep in the reception and storage area for several months, while renting these units for around $200/night. We were constantly in investment and growth mode. It was an incredibly exciting time for us and Tulum; sometimes stressful, but that is expected when growing a business.

* * *

Tips

- If you don't have the capital, don't give up: be creative to find it.

- Remember, most people will invest in YOU, not just your project.

- It's important to reinvest in your business. The more you invest, the faster you can grow.

- Live a humble lifestyle while growing your company so that you can invest more; then, your growth will become exponential very quickly.

5

AIRBNB VALUE-ADDED SERVICES

Love the life you live. Live the life you love.

—Bob Marley

When we started our rental business, the renters would ask us several questions before their arrival to the property. Tulum is an area unknown to most people, and most are first-time visitors. The first add-on amenity we started, which was the easiest to put into place, was picking our guests up at the airport. We personally drove our guests to and from the airport in an old 1995 Ford Explorer for a standard rate of $75 each way. Suddenly, we had a new source of revenue, and, more than that, it was a positive and memorable experience for our guests. They loved it. The transportation service with other companies was around $120–$150 round trip. As an added benefit, this was a great way to meet and create a relationship with our renters, beginning the minute they arrive and before they step foot on the property. This added amenity guaranteed a positive review, and guests paid us while we collected valuable insights into their expectations and desires at our locations. And driving them back to the airport, we could get feedback on areas we could improve; also, it gave us the opportunity to smooth over any situation so that our renters left happy. They loved it. And this VIP airport pickup and drop off almost always guaranteed a great review.

Next, our guests would ask where to rent a car for their own transportation during their stay with us. When renting a vehicle, especially in Mexico, insurance, hidden pricing additions, and the local laws would concern our guests. So, we came up with a new amenity. Why don't we just pick up the guests, give them the car, and then charge that guest a daily rental fee for use of our 1995 Ford Explorer. We could charge our guests $400–$500 per week to rent a vehicle, and they would gladly pay for the convenient and trusted service. If we picked guests up at the airport, we'd offer to rent the car to them for the week. Nico purchased the

1995 Ford Explorer when living in San Louis Potosí, Mexico, for $2,500, then we rented the car for $500 per week; as you can see, it was a great return on investment for us!

Our guests were happy to pay for the additional amenities. With the car rental service success, we determined that purchasing more cars to rent to guests was a lucrative investment. We began buying vehicles and accumulated three or four different vans and cars. At first, we were a little embarrassed driving a minivan around, but when we realized they are great because they work for big groups, fit lots of luggage, and people pay more for them. When we drove our guests from the airport, we'd advertise the car for rent, and more often than not, the guests would choose to rent the vehicle for their stay. It turned into a positive revenue source. Not only was it positive cashflow for the business but also guests loved the service, which helped their overall experience and, of course, our online guest reviews.

Our goal was to have enough cars so that all our guests could use them if needed. We were able to get an official license to rent cars, since we had been doing it under the table, which was a bit risky. This license costed around $15,000, and when we finally got it, we added, a Smart car and a Nissan Leaf electric vehicle to the fleet. However, at this time we started growing too fast, and everything was quite difficult to manage, so we basically put the car-rental option on hold.

Our guests consistently asked about a private chef service or grocery delivery service to their property. We don't like to say no, so we looked for chefs in the Tulum area. We found a great chef, and we began to offer this service to renters: guests with Airbnb value convenient food options when relaxing and enjoying the property. I created a website called groceryplaya.com, which had a complete online grocery store and an option to reserve chef service as well. This was my first time doing anything such as website creation, but it was fun and also cool to see the online store working, cash flow coming in, and more guests happy. At first, the idea was for our guests, but we did open it up to the entire vacation rental market. Once we grew more, we ended up just providing this service for our guests.

All these services helped the company grow. Our guests loved it and gladly gave us great reviews. We bonded with our guests while we uncovered what else would make their stay at our property an unforgettable experience. We provided personalized tours of the area to our guests. By interacting with our guests and asking questions, we were able to give a tour that fit perfectly with the guests' wants and expectations. We also provided free bikes at each property so that our guests could explore the area on their own time. We added one new unexpected amenity after another, so each experience for the next guest was better than the last.

As hosts we always maintained a responsive attitude to our guests' every like or dislike, and we hustled to provide what was, in their mind, missing. If we ensured that their experience was unforgettable, and we bonded with our guests, they would leave a great review, tell their friends and family, and want to comeback. And if you follow these steps naturally, the money will always come in the end. That was our attitude and still is to this day.

We didn't worry about costs and expenses. Providing multiple amenities and personalized services was a differentiator. Instead of doing the bare minimum, hosts providing comprehensive vacation experiences has become more common with bed-and-breakfast lodgings or Airbnb rentals. At the time, no other hosts offered the types and quality of services provided for our guests at our properties. It showed in our occupancy rate: we were always booked solid. In our first couple years, our properties were always over 90 percent rented! Our goal was to both sleep in our 250-square-foot reception/storage/laundry room; one on the sofa bed, the other on the ground. Those painful and uncomfortable nights' sleep never felt so good!

We soon became guest service professionals and experts. We were the concierges, providing transportation and even eating dinner at local restaurants with our guests. In our listings, we asked future guests questions about how they envisioned their stay, and then we studied the responses to learn what our renters wanted most; for example, we weren't aggressive advertising tours, but if a guest indicated a desire for a personalized tour, we'd definitely offer it to them. We'd tell people all the services we offer, and after they made a reservation, we'd offer our base services. The more services we provided, the more our guests would order them! When our guests asked about an unoffered service, we'd provide it if we could. After the guest checked out, we'd ask how we could improve, and then provide a better experience for their next stay—or the best experience possible to future guests. Before starting this business, we had no professional experience in hospitality, but we definitely became experts through our hands-on 24/7/365 experience and dedication.

* * *

TIPS

- Concentrate on guest experience more than the income. The income will come automatically, and lots of it.

- Think about how you can grow your revenue with parallel businesses.

- You can become an expert at something with hard work and lots of sweat.

- Your business won't become successful overnight; it takes lots of hard work by the founder.

6

RUNNING AN AIRBNB, BECOMING A SUPERHOST, AND MAKING MONEY

You only live once, but if you do it right, once
is enough.

—Mae West

Los Amigos substantially grew once the first
seven-unit condo building was built. We now had
seven units in one area and a house in the same
neighborhood. Providing that personal touch
became more difficult since the company's size
more than doubled with the condo building. We
were hands on, and we only had few employees.
With only one or two cleaners working for us at a
time, we were the reception. And if maintenance
was needed, we'd personally fix the issue and would

call somebody else in extreme cases only. Nico loves telling the story about how many toilets he has unclogged personally, and the guests are surprised and embarrassed at the same time. Imagine your host seeing what you left in the toilet, and then driving you to the airport the next day!

From unclogging toilets to cleaning the pool to landscaping, we did everything. We were a two-man show. From the very moment guests arrived, we'd be on the clock, offering 24/7 service, from picking them up to dropping them off at the airport. We were always biking from one property to the next, running around like crazy. We did it all—we knew from reviews we were doing a great job, and even though we never had a true break, it made us feel good knowing that we offered a great service and that our guests left very happy.

Most people thought we lived like guests at our properties. We'd get many questions, such as "What do you do here in Tulum?" or "What do you do for work?" They didn't realize how hard we worked, and that renting the vacation properties was a viable and profitable business model, not just a setup for us to laze about. We took the job seriously, we dressed the part, and we were very professional:

it all paid off. Once we got up to 19 units, we had to hire more people because the amount of work became overwhelming. We hired a maintenance person and a couple more cleaners, and eventually we hired a receptionist. We were reluctant to hire staff, afraid the quality of service would diminish if we didn't personally provide it, but we wanted to grow and so we had to risk it. The scariest moment was letting someone else respond to our guests on Airbnb. There is always a certain touch that an owner adds to communication that is not easy for an employee to replicate. We trained constantly, and employees got really close to our response style, giving the right experience to our guests.

Managing employees came with its own difficulties. We grew attached and we sometimes cried when we had to let them go or when an employee wanted to leave. At first it's hard to deal with, but as you grow and work, you learn this is just normal, and even the best and most loyal employees will leave one day (or even steal from you). But as the company grew, employee hiring and termination was a reality we had to get used to as business owners. In the context of running a business, the health of the business must come first. Hiring is easy, but you must fire quickly and decisively when necessary. Sometimes employees stay around too long because it's unpleasant taking away a worker's livelihood. But, poor employees resulted in more complaints and recurring issues. We had two options: train them more, and hope they improve, or terminate the employee. Retraining is often not an option, especially when the employee has a pattern of not following instructions, so we have to resort to something quicker and not be emotional about the decision.

Owning, Managing, and Being a Superhost

For several years now we have been recognized as the top host in the region because we focus on customer service and experience. Also, we now have over 5000 5-star reviews. which is not easy to achieve if you're just managing your own places and not others. We attentively listened to our clients, and we took every word seriously. If a pillow wasn't comfortable or if a guest requested we should provide two coffees instead of one, then we remedied the issue. We endeavored to make all imperfections perfect—that's how we built our business's reputation.

We offered as many amenities and services necessary to give guests a great experience. Each review helped us to polish our company's model. We could have been laid back, hired people to do our work, and made decent profits, but that wasn't enough. There's always room for improvement, and it brings us great satisfaction when the improvements make a better vacation experience for our guests.

We strove to perfect our standards and build on our unique business model. Airbnb made us part of their VIP program; they wanted to work with us and have direct contact. They also invited us to the international convention in Los Angeles in November 2016. We were invited to represent all of Mexico! We went to many special functions and VIP events where the top hosts in the world gathered along with one of the owners of Airbnb and other executives. At these gatherings, our reputation preceded; some of the attendees had even bought real estate property from us because they knew the returns we were getting were amazing.

While we were in one of the meetings in Los Angeles with other Airbnb hosts, we realized that we're the only host that owns and manages all our units. Most Airbnb hosts with that many units were property managers, handling 50–100 properties with various owners. We were owners of this magnitude able to manage our own properties and to maintain a Superhost rating. Airbnb said that once you have a certain number of units, it's almost impossible to be a Superhost because of unforeseeable or uncontrollable factors like cancellations or unavoidable issues with staff that make it impossible to maintain a rating above 90 percent. There are four criteria a Superhost excels in, and we crushed all of them. The most difficult is to have an average of 4.8 out of 5.0 stars. The next most complicated criterion is 0 cancelations by the host. The last 2 for us are the easiest: you must have a 90 percent response rate and at least 10 stays in the year. We usually have over a 98 percent response rate, and over 1500 Airbnb stays per year. Still, to maintain the Superhost status is very difficult because there's so many things that can be out of your control when your operation becomes large.

MAKING MONEY WITH AIRBNB

I never thought it would be possible to earn $1,000,000 building a business around Airbnb and vacation rentals. As a new business, you can't expect to ever be so profitable and especially so quickly. In about four years, our revenue was just under a million dollars. We were paying ourselves modestly, but growing profits and reinvesting most of it into the company. We also had a few small investors along the way because relying on our own money wasn't enough. From the beginning until now, we have invested well over $1,000,000 of profit back into the business.

To get significant profits quickly, you need to own the units. Basically, you need investors or a small amount of investor money or your own capital. Our business strategy involved all three, plus reinvesting. With that type of formula, it's sufficient to build a business in a small growing, developing city. This business model works best in foreign countries outside the United States, but it's possible anywhere in the world if done correctly. There's a lot of options in the world where you can start investing a small amount of money and grow a business. As you grow, always reinvest into your company. If you follow this strategy, it's possible to reach $1 million in revenue in about 3-5 years.

For people just interested in making a modest income by becoming an entrepreneur or managing someone else's property, there's a couple of models that could work. You could rent a unit and then sublease the unit. We've followed this model a few times when we started out to make extra cash flow. We made a decent amount, and since you don't own the unit, there's little risk involved. You just have to find the right situation: an owner that allows subleasing (or never learns about it), and an attractive area. For example, we rented a unit with a one-year contract. Then we put the listings on Airbnb, or other websites, to find vacation goers and short-term renters. The guest paid hotel rates and we dealt with the landlord or the owners of the property. If we had a unit with a $1,000 rent, we'd usually make between $2,000 to $3,000 a month, leaving with about a 100 percent monthly net profit.

After investing in our first house, Casa Los Amigos, in Tulum, we were making good money. We were probably averaging a net monthly income of $1,500 each, which is about 3 times more than the average salary in Tulum, Mexico. So, when we started Condos Los Amigos, I was already thinking about retiring, but we just kept going and money wasn't the motivator. The rental business is more like a passion to us—we don't think about the work as work, and opportunities just seem to roll in.

* * *

TIPS

- If your business has ratings and reviews, it's important that you are on top for the most success.

- If you do Airbnb, you need to be a Superhost.

- Don't settle for OK, you can always do better and improve.

- Reinvest, reinvest, reinvest.

7

RUNNING PROJECTS AND HIRING STAFF

If you think you can do a thing or think you
can't do a thing, you're right.

—Henry Ford

Prior to our first venture, we didn't realize the
practical strength of a business partner. We started
as friends. We're both casual and had a lot of the
same interests in traveling, and we both possess an
entrepreneurial spirit.

We both wished to prioritize sustainability in
our land and property development; sustainability
would give our business a distinctive quality. We
naturally partnered up and began a very basic
operation, and each success built on the next. We
both did everything in the beginning and learned

our unique strengths and weaknesses as the obstacles arose.

It is critical that both partners understand every aspect of the business; however, as we grew, we realized we were spreading ourselves too thin. We were each trying to do everything. Doing our best to be in every meeting together, discussing every topic together. We soon realized that we needed to divide the tasks based on our strengths. So, we'd decide who would best perform in a given task to enhance the business. We were able to efficiently solve problems and adjust our business rapidly when needed. We respected and trusted each other's views and strengths and allowed the other to make difficult decisions on his own. When you're seeking a business partner, you need someone who is reliable and who is strong where you're weak, but most of importantly, someone who you can trust.

We came across a book titled *Rocket Fuel*, coauthored by Mark Winters and Gino Wickman. This book was transformational for us, particularly the ideas of the integrator and the visionary. We realized the dual roles were a prime example of our relationship. Realizing this allowed us to split duties based on our individual strengths. Nico was more of the personality and face of the company in his role (and had crazy ideas): the visionary.

I work best behind the scenes as the integrator and operator. I'm typically more involved in the legal, financial , and operational details. I put Nico in his place with his crazy ideas, but when he comes up with a great one, that's when it's my job to make it happen. This worked really well for us. That seemed to really be one of the key factors of success for our business. We each learned our own unique strengths and applied them to help the business, instead of us each doing the same task or occupying both roles.

RUNNING PROJECTS

Completing several projects at the same time, which included hiring architects and contractors, was always a highly stressful process for me, even though my background is in construction management. Having studied in the US, I became very familiar with proper standards, rules, and processes in construction. Early on, it became clear that the processes were different in Mexico. In Mexico, especially in the southern regions, there are many opportunities where you can quickly open a business and hire employees or contractors.

So, in 2016 with a vision for another house, we hired an in-house architect directly to our payroll who would help us design and build the property. Our architect helped us to hire labor crews of carpenters, masonry, electricians, and other tradespeople.

The Glass House, or *Villa Vidrio*, was the first property that we managed the building process completely ourselves. The whole front of the house was seamless glass, which was a more beautiful and aesthetic design. Most people we told our design idea to said, "No, don't do that. It's too expensive" (even the glass company that sold us this expensive glass!). We listened, but decided to go against their opinions and to go for it. You can't take someone's limiting beliefs or opinions as facts. Make your own decisions and take responsibility for the outcome.

As we were building The Glass House, we remained open to the idea of selling the house if a buyer came along. We could either operate it like we had planned, or we could sell it and operate it if the owner wished. Keeping an open mind gave us options. Since we had a lot of guests, we'd ask if someone was interested in buying the house. We casually brought it up to guests when they asked us about investing, "Hey, we have a house. You want to check it out?" One gentleman who looked at the property under construction laughed at our timeline and said, "If you finish this house in two months, I'll buy the house from you."

Needless to say, we sold the house to him and we still manage it to this day. We realized the benefits of this system: building the properties ourselves and having control over the building and design process, then selling the properties and managing the units. This worked well for us. There were approximately 10–12 full-time workers in the construction group. From there, just like in the United States, we hired subcontractors based on the type of specialty work needed on the project. We never wanted to sell anything because all the properties were cash cows, but we thought we could explore another business opportunity: real estate development.

CONTROL OF THE CONSTRUCTION QUALITY

We wanted to continue building more projects and growing at a fast pace, but we realized we could grow faster if we had our own staff. The problem with faster growth is that we were at the mercy of the architect and builder, who were part of the same company in our case, and not under our management. We weren't always their first priority. Given my background in construction management, we wanted to explore being our own contractor for each of the properties and projects we developed going forward.

We realized that at the speed we were growing and the opportunities ahead of us, we needed to grow at a quicker pace. That's exactly what we did. We continued with the architect that we hired from Craigslist to build The Glass house; the architect stayed on and worked on the design of new future projects. The construction group involved just Nico, the architect, and me at this time. Once we began our next project, which was bigger than our previous project, it became necessary to hire a superintendent and an additional architect and engineer. The superintendent was responsible now for hiring labor on each new project. We didn't subcontract any further so that we could control the quality of our projects; now, the main professional construction team who worked on our projects were our direct employees and part of our team.

Hiring Direct Staff

We found the overall costs of the projects were lower when we stopped dealing with a third-party architect or contractor, or both. This structure removed the middleman since we had the superintendent take care of these tasks. There's definitely more work for you as the business owner, but by directly employing workers, we received responses faster, and quick and reliable communication made a massive difference for production. The answers to project inquiries were quickly given, there was more transparency on every project, and the costs were reduced. Having all this information at our fingertips began to abolish some of the doubts we originally had.

As we grew, challenges arose, as they do with a rapidly expanding company. We became more involved with authorities, the government, and local jurisdictions for the area, which was a true learning experience. Also, it is vitally important to be highly involved with your company's finances to ensure you can meet the additional payroll, along with learning how to properly manage all the employees.

* * *

TIPS

- Trust is the most important thing in any business relationship.

- Try and realize who is the integrator and who is the visionary as soon as possible, and work on your strengths.

- Go for what you believe in and know, instead of always listening to others.

- Taking risks is a great way to have massive success in business.

- Stay involved in the accounting of your company and don't just trust the accounting professionals that you hire.

8

TAKING RISKS
AND BUYING A HECTARE!

It always seems impossible until it's done.

—Nelson Mandela

Our typical model was to buy a small piece of land, about 280 square meters (3,000 square feet). We'd build the property and rent it on the vacation rental platforms, mainly Airbnb, then use the cash flow to buy another piece of land and build the next property. That's how our first projects went. And it worked well, with no stress, just reinvesting the money, and a few investors early on.

One day while searching for land, we found a plot of land that was 10,000 square meters, or one hectare. A hectare measures at approximately 2.47 acres. Developing a piece of land a hectare in size was never planned. For us, this was huge! We never imagined being able to buy a piece of land this big, on our own at least. Now let's explain how we got here . . .

At the time, the market was considered a seller's market and land prices continued to rise so much we couldn't find land within our budget for the size of land we usually developed. Little did we know at this time in 2016 land was actually still very cheap. That's when we decided to look at bigger parcels of land where we could build a bigger project— bigger meaning 550–930 square meters (about 6,000–10,000 square feet), or 2–3 times bigger than our normal land. We couldn't seem to find the right land this time. We'd make offers, but they wouldn't go through. So, we looked at all our options and found a private community which included full infrastructure, such as roads, drainage, and electricity, already in place, which wasn't common in other areas of Tulum. The area was called Aldea Zama, which also had a financing program for their lands. This was one option that we could consider: putting a down payment on the land, then have monthly payments where we could try and pay with our cash flow. At this point we kept looking.

We had a budget in mind. With the working capital we had, we'd have around $100,000 as a down payment on the most attractive land we could find. So, we continued looking. We went around to different agencies, which all had different offers. This is typical in Tulum, as there is no global public listing agency such as the MLS (Multiple Listing Service) in the US.

We eventually found this piece of land, which we began calling The Hectare. The land was way bigger than we imagined; in fact, it was about 30 times the size of lots we typically purchased. This was in an area that wasn't developed, and only accessible by jungle roads. The area is called region 15 or *la veleta*. The good news was that we also had 2 of our other projects on the same street, so we knew the area was great. The land sale price at the time was $350,000, which for us was way more than we had ever spent on land. (Remember, our normal land purchase was around $30,000.) We didn't have that kind of money sitting around, but we knew this was an amazing opportunity. We didn't know yet what we were going to do with it, but we made an offer. After negotiating with the owner, our offer was finally accepted, and we made a deal where we could make a down payment of 20 percent and pay the remaining balance after two months. It's not typical to get financing, so most purchases are all cash. During these 2 months, we didn't have the capital. We did have some different options, though. I was against going through with this purchase without having the money secured before putting down the deposit, but Nico was insistent that we'd figure it out. I was definitely nervous, but Nico always liked taking crazy risks! This was probably one of the biggest risks we took to date, as we put down a nonrefundable deposit of around $70,000 with the hopes of finding the rest of the money in just 2 months. But we knew the land was too good to pass up.

Later, around the same time, we made a deal for the land in Aldea Zama. We were all out of capital, since we spent the majority on the down payment of The Hectare, so we went to a potential investment partner, who then paid the down payment for the land. We did a joint venture: fifty-fifty on the costs and proceeds, but having this partner join us and pay the down payment was the only way we could expand more at this time. From there we were able to design a project, start preselling which is something that was quite new at the time, and use the money from the presales to pay for the rest of the land. In this creative way, we didn't have to put down out of pocket capital from the company. We kept expanding in creative ways, which was also a key factor in our rapid growth. This project, called the Highline, was very successful and sold about 100 percent in less than 6 months. Therefore, we were able to use the money from the sales to pay for the construction. A complete project with zero out of pocket!

It's not very common in Mexico to get a loan on land or houses, which is common in the United States, and other parts of the world. In most cases, Mexico's real estate and land development is a cash market. We really needed to have the money for this particular project. We kept our options open for the worst-case scenarios. The first option was to sell The Glass House to obtain funding; the second option was to obtain bank financing, which was very difficult as well; and the third option involved getting a silent partner, which we weren't sure we wanted to do because of the amount we'd have to give up with that arrangement. The most likely solution was to get 1–2 people to invest in our project. Amazingly, a couple days before the last payment was due, we sold The Glass House and got a small loan from the bank. We were able to finish the deal on April 21, 2016; we closed the deal, and everything working out perfectly. Phew, that was a close one!

TAKING RISKS

In our partnership, Nico is more of the risk-taker and strong visionary. I'm more calculated and conservative. This helps us keep the balance. Our entire business is built on risks. With the nature of our business, it is the only way to be successful, and especially at such a fast pace. We started with very little, but now we were in a place where people would ask us how we knew where to invest, what to build, or how we trusted others. Everything we did along the way was risky, but we made deals with people we didn't know so that we could grow. We put up a lot of cash, but we made a lot of cash as well.

We bought property, land, and ran a business without having the money. On many deals we struggled finding investors or direct financing and began most projects with not much money in the bank. We eventually raised the necessary funds over time to have working capital to fund our own projects. That is the key. A lot of people are very conservative. But, in general, you must take risks. At this point in our journey, we both didn't have many worries, which made making risky decisions easier. Also, we live a very humble lifestyle, so we could take greater risks. Not everyone is willing to do that.

After we bought the land, the next risk was to rent an office. We had never thought of renting an office before, because we had always worked on-site at our properties. Eventually, we rented an office on the main street of Tulum, starting with one table and two employees. From there we started hiring and designing more projects. We just kept growing and moving forward. We continued to invest back into the business and to fund new projects with the last project's profits.

Smart Investment

As we were risking bigger money, the company was expanding and seeing more success. We thought we had finally discovered the secret formula when we made that first investment back in Tulum. At that time, nobody knew about the area; it was kind of unheard of in the real estate and vacation rental industry. We foresaw the potential for growth in the region that nobody else did. Our rentals in Tulum were an instantaneous success, and we easily recuperated our investment within the first two years. When we traveled, we realized 90 percent of the world's population hadn't heard of Tulum, and this location was in high demand, but barely developed. We knew we struck gold, so we decided to go all in. Any money put into Tulum would have a healthy return.

Purchasing land is a reliable investment because land is physical, is limited, and will always retain value. Investing in land is one of the most solid investments. Even today, whatever happens in the market, you'll always have the land. We figured, even if the market crashed, we could just put a trailer on the land and wait until the market bounced back or build what we could with the little money we had remaining.

Land is a tangible investment: it won't just disappear like stocks in a failing company. Compare buying land and paying cash with buying a house with a small down payment, as most people do, which is a much bigger risk. If, and when, the market corrects or, worse, crashes, then you'll be left with a big problem as you'll then owe more money on your home than it's worth, and probably need to short sale or foreclose. We paid in full, which was less risky because we had no debt. We started with a small risk, relatively, but we invested all the money that we had, plus a little more. That small investment—even though it was all we had— was easier to recuperate. We took our first risk, thinking that if it doesn't rent, at least we have a paid-off house for our families in the Caribbean where we can visit anytime. We only became riskier with our investments because we had so much confidence in the area and with the return on investment. After that first risk and success, our risks kept getting bigger but more calculated.

Reinvesting Everything

When we met backpacking, we both had had successful but unfulfilling careers; material desire wasn't the force that drove our entrepreneurial ambition. We were very humble, always looking for the cheapest hostels and food. We were responsible with our money, but we did travel a lot and spend money on experiences, such as scuba diving and cultural experiences.

When we started our business, we lived in a small apartment with an extra room. The extra room was always rented, and even when one of us went on vacation to visit family, his room would be rented out. We always reinvested what little extra money we had into the next project. As new entrepreneurs, it's important to concentrate on the company and not live, or desire to live, extravagantly. The car we shared when we started our first venture was very old. We rode bikes everywhere, so investing in a new car wasn't necessary for us. We only bought another car so that we could have it rented by our guests. As we grew, we purchased a Tesla Model X as an investment for the company, to create an unforgettable experience for our guests—they love it.

Even though the company has grown and become successful, we focus on working hard and reinvesting every penny: this will pay us tenfold in the future. We don't need much money beyond having enough to eat, live, and travel modestly. The satisfaction of our company's success, and sharing with people our story, is more than sufficient. Also, the fulfillment we feel in seeing how happy our guests are with their experiences is more than enough.

Before traveling to Mexico, we both saw our peers working into old age, frustrated and unhappy. That is not how we envisioned our futures. We're both very independent and adventurous and didn't want to sacrifice precious time for a hated job. So, reinvesting in the company wasn't only good business but compatible with our future goals: to cultivate a life of freedom and independence!

* * *

TIPS

- Keep pushing forward with ideas and projects until the right one falls into place.

- Taking risks are very important for an entrepreneur or new business.

- Start small, do your due diligence, then go big!

9

DEVELOPING TULUM, SUSTAINABILITY, AND PROFIT

Who looks outside, dreams; who looks inside, awakes.

—Carl Jung

Tulum is now known as one of the best tourist destinations in the world. There has never been a better time to invest in a piece of real estate or land in Tulum: real estate is affordable and the return on investment is lucrative. The value of land in Tulum is expected to appreciate greatly in the short- and long-term. Nothing is guaranteed, but smart entrepreneurs take calculated risks. As such, return on investment will be likely for any entrepreneur willing to invest in land in Tulum. Investing in real estate in Tulum isn't like gambling in a lottery club. Now, there are modern and state of the art infrastructures, both foreign and government investors, as well as year-round tourism, which make the region an ideal place to invest in.

CENTRAL PARK TULUM

Central Park Tulum is a luxurious holiday getaway. This condo hotel was our first large scale project, and it was built on The Hectare. We first started designing on a quarter of the land and we were going to save the rest of the land for later, but then decided to build 1 large project with amazing amenities, and then later we can buy more land if successful. We started preselling units before construction began in May 2016, and we sold 100 percent of the first phase of 24 units in less than a month. Our main focus was studios: 400 square foot hotel rooms with a kitchenette. We also offered something unheard of: a 10 percent guarantee on ROI annually. We knew this was easy to achieve with our current operating experience, but for the rest of the world this was unheard of. These things went like hotcakes! We delivered these units in April 2017, less than 1 year, which is unheard of in this business. Tourists can choose to either stay in a small studio-sized apartment or a larger suite or even a three-bedroom penthouse with a rooftop glass bottom pool. The property is self-sufficient and sustainable. It has solar panels on the roofs, an amazing smart solar flower made in Austria in the common areas, and even the water is recycled and filtered using a very advanced reverse osmosis system new to development in the area. Central Park is the only property in Tulum that provides Tesla destination chargers. Some of the attractions close to the Central Park include the famous cenotes, which are underground canal systems of fresh water that run through the entire region; the world famous Tulum ruins, which are now visited by more than 2 million tourists annually; the world class beaches, which are just a few minutes' drive away; and a new Guggenheim museum at Azulik hotel on the beach.

Central Park also offers some world class amenities for our guests: two large kid-friendly pools with sun lounging areas, a three-story gym with a 30-foot-high indoor rock climbing wall and juice bar, a healthy concept restaurant called Sugarfree, which is inspired by our vision and style, and a five-star luxury spa. All our properties have bicycles and airport transportation for hire. There are also youth and other family-friendly activities available, and we give restaurant and tour suggestions in our guidebooks and directly with our concierges.

When designing Central Park, we wanted to put incredible amenities in to make sure that all the guests would have an incredible experience. We liked to build things that we knew were necessary from our hands-on experience with our guests and our living there as well. Tulum at the time didn't even have one gym with air conditioning! Nico was Mr. Millennium in Germany when he was 18, which was the biggest bodybuilding competition during the time, and has always been a workout junkie, so having his own gym was certainly a dream of his. So, we decided why not build an incredible 3-level gym! As well Tulum didn't have a luxury spa and we knew this was a need for Tulum going forward, so we did lots of research and built an incredible luxury spa. Also, since diabetes is one of the biggest killers in Mexico, we wanted to create a restaurant that provides healthy options to our guests.

Central Park also provides very classy room amenities. These amenities include a kitchenette, a microwave, a refrigerator, a flat-screen TV, a sitting and relaxing area, and housekeeping services. We wanted to provide hotel amenities so that our guests can enjoy their time in Tulum. Central Park is now surrounded by other popular restaurants, such as Burrito Amor, Raw Love, and many others in town. Guests are a few minutes' drive from famous beach restaurants such as Hartwood and Casa Jaguar. Also, there are the endless, amazing beach clubs, such as our very own Los Amigos Beach Club, or you can check out our neighbors Casa Malca, known as the Pablo Escobar property, or Be Tulum. There are always events with famous chefs, such as in 2017 when René Redzepi from the restaurant Noma did a dinner for $700/person and it sold out every night for 1 month. Based on our guests' interests, we can have our staff make the best recommendations for them to enjoy their night out.

Yes, I said our own beach club. We always looked at beach options, but the beach is very limited and exclusive and prices are very elevated. But as we kept growing and building more and more apartments, we figured it would make more sense for this investment so that our guests would have a place to go. In Tulum, the beach clubs aren't always that easy to access unless you are guests there, so we found the solution and were able to land a deal to rent and operate a beach club!

When we started building and selling Central Park Tulum in 2016, we began to feel the buzz in the area. We bought as much land as we could with our capital. We were having trouble raising money at this time, since most investors that we knew were too slow or too conservative, so we bought as much as we could handle—we knew the area was going to increase in value after the completion of our project. As we foresaw, the area rose in value, and since we were the first project in the area, the rewards were significant. Now there are over 100 projects, and of course the land costs have gone up tremendously.

REASONS FOR DEVELOPMENT

In the underdeveloped parts of Tulum, there are still great opportunities to invest and to develop affordability. We believe investing here is better than stock market investments, or even better than investing in real estate in developed areas. Other than in Tulum, there are hundreds of underdeveloped areas to invest in land and to build condo hotels around the world. We saw the opportunity in Tulum. Below are a few reasons investing in an underdeveloped area is great and what you can look for in other areas that have potential.

You'll greatly profit by investing in a piece of land in places poised for future growth, like Tulum. This happens only by waiting and selling when the correct time comes or building property on the land into something useful. Some clients have reaped over 100 percent returns on properties purchased from our company. This has happened in less than 2 years in some cases as the growth in Tulum and the region has really taken off. People have said several times that the project Central Park Tulum in 2016/2017 was really the tipping point of the real estate market in Tulum.

The Riviera Maya area in Mexico covers over 80 miles along the Caribbean Coast. There are a high number of tourists visiting this area. Tulum is located about one hour's drive south of the Cancun International Airport. The number of tourists that vacation on this Caribbean coastline increase annually. Playa Del Carmen and Puerto Aventuras also form part of this coastline. Tulum alone is not able to satisfy this market since there is a deficit in hotels, condos, and any type of lodging facility. Years ago there was a plan to put an international airport in Tulum. As this was positive for some and negative for others, it also created a buzz. In the end, the plan was squashed; instead, they are building a large project called the Mayan Train, which will connect the entire Yucatan peninsula and Quintana Roo states together by the train. It's estimated to cost over $6.5 billion.

Development in Tulum is still in its initial stages. This makes it an exceptional value for land developers and investors alike. The tourism market is not yet flooded; so, there is room for growth and development. According to *International Living*, "Tulum is competing for the title of the fastest-growing Mexican city and is continuing to present a robust opportunity to buy real estate, and it is discounted for those who are using U.S. dollars as capital."

Most real estate investments require a lot of property maintenance and upkeep. The best thing about investing in a property with Los Amigos is that we will also help maintain it and/or have a great partner company to help you, so it remains a hands-off investment. You can also just own raw land and sell it after it appreciates; in this case, you would just pay a yearly property tax. In both cases it is simple for foreigners to own in Tulum with either a bank trust or starting a company.

* * *

TIPS

- Always try to provide incredible guest experiences in your business model.

- Cross-selling is a great way to make more income and have happier guests.

- Living in the area is the best market research you can do.

- Look to invest in underdeveloped areas in the world.

10

BECOMING SUSTAINABLE AND A MARKET LEADER

Try not to become a man of success but rather to become a man of value.

—Albert Einstein

DIFFERENCE BETWEEN SUSTAINABILITY AND GOING GREEN

We were both passionate about sustainability and realized the business importance of embracing sustainability and green energy manufacturing. Even before we met and started doing business together, we were both connected with sustainability in a big way. I am LEED Accredited and worked on LEED projects in the US; also, my family had solar panels on the rooftop and installed other energy saving options. Nico had a very large private solar plant in Germany, and he was even interested in doing business in Mexico with solar before we even met. Efficiency and competitiveness, as well as huge profits, can be achieved when organizations adopt sustainable and green practices. So, this is not just a contemporary practice to implement. Not only is sustainability a trendy practice but manufacturers who practice it have realized both short-term and long-term financial improvements.

There is not much difference between sustainability and going *green*. Green mostly refers to a single part of production or process that doesn't harm the environment—for example, making a certain product out of recycled materials. *Sustainability* is how the organization performs its various functions. Both the logistics and the production teams have to be involved.

An example of a sustainable practice is when you acquire from abroad a green product that has been recycled; however, if the mode of transportation used to deliver that product is harmful to the environment, then sustainable principles were generally overlooked. Manufacturers should pay attention to both green and sustainable business practices if they not only want to attract environmentally conscious consumers but want to reduce their companies impact on the environment.

There are a variety of ways you can make a positive impact if you adopt a sustainability focus. An organization can easily reduce the expenses associated with water and energy. They can implement various ways of improvement to deal with these expenses, like reverse osmosis and solar technology. However, these cost-effective mechanisms are long-term and can only be realized on an annual basis. Costs on electricity can be controlled by adopting energy-efficient lighting and controlling lighting levels by the demand of your production schedule. Any leakages should be identified—they are a waste of energy that can be identified through equipment inspections.

A company can also change its product and supply packaging. This can lead to cost-effective measures and create more space within the facility. Implementing solar and wind energy and using equipment and machinery that are energy friendly can help retain energy. By recycling and avoiding much paperwork, you can reduce supply costs. A company can achieve a good reputation from customers who are also cautious about the environment. This will result in more sales by targeting sustainability and green-conscious customers. Once these customers purchase from you, the word will get out about your values as a company over time. You tend to attract more customers by letting them know how your company operates. This results in better sales. For manufacturers looking forward to acquiring government contracts, their green manufacturing standards have to be top-notch.

There are various options of tax credits and rebates offered at either the federal or state level for sustainable manufacturers. They are all business friendly. This, of course, depends on the country and local state tax laws, so be sure you consult with your legal and tax team about the best strategy obtaining tax incentives for sustainable practices. A sustainability-focused company is also attractive for employees, who often believe in a company's mission if they approve of how the company operates. So, when employees come together and embrace green and sustainable methods, it results in great teamwork and daily improvement.

Through sustainability, innovation gets generated. For example, at times, you may want to reduce the amount of scrap or increase the amount of waste to recycling while manufacturing. The engineers and mechanics working in a firm may often generate new ideas when sustainability is appended to a classic problem, such as waste management.

While profitability may be realized within your company, your mode of operation may turn out to be different. You are actually making an impact on society and culture with these sustainability plans and focus with your company. By practicing changes, the carbon footprint will be reduced and the number of toxins dispersed to the environment will be diminished. Future generations will thus have air free from any toxins, clean freshwater, and numerous renewable energy channels.

Becoming a Market Leader

Being a market leader does not come easily. It requires strategic planning and lots of hard work. Below are some guidelines start-ups can implement to be among the top in their field.

Most players in a given market are well established. Narrow down on a specific niche for your market; it is more difficult to try and serve a broad market because nothing will set you apart from other companies. Never channel your energy on how you want to battle it out with larger public market companies. Rather, look for a small unidentified market and specialize in this product or service. It's easier to become a leader in a small unsaturated niche.

Competition is everywhere, including a niche market. To be a leader, you have to do things that your competitors aren't. Seth Godin in his book *Purple Cow* emphasizes transforming your business by being remarkable. A standout product is a key to success. The Purple Cow model is illustrated by both Google and Apple. In 1984 computer manufacturers had already saturated the market. This is the year that Apple manufactured Macintosh. The company mainly focused on the look of the computer and user experience. Google was launched in 1998. It focused on how best it would rank in search results and by creating a user-friendly platform. To be a leader, identify what can make a business unique, consider what your competitors haven't yet done, and take a product and look at it from a different angle.

Don't waste your time trying to come up with a perfect, new product. Rather, focus on continually improving an existing model. Always remember that there is never a perfect product. After submitting your product to the market, listen to what customers are saying about it, what they want to be done differently, and any negative issue, or positive review. Always accept changes, be creative, and don't lose focus trying to beat your competitors but listen to the consumers.

Customers have the power to either make or break a company. Customer satisfaction has been one of the primary focuses of our company, from the beginning. You can use social media and technology as a tool to engage with consumers and potential consumers. Start by surveying and talking to one customer, and then talk to another. You'll be amazed at what you can discover to improve your customer experience. Just like we did.

Then focus on building up your online reviews. Today more than ever before, online reviews and comments is the most important tool for marketing your product. If you have negative reviews, make sure to take seriously the comments, make it better, and communicate with these clients. To make a good product, negative reviews should inform its improvements. Communication is the key, and make your marketing unique. Also, use advertisement posts so that customers get familiar with your products. We rely mostly on Instagram and Facebook, but it's important to be in as many different social media and marketing platforms as possible—this is a changing industry all the time.

* * *

Tips

- Having sustainability in your business model and vision has never been more important than in today's world.

- Strive to become a market leader in a special niche or area that you see opportunity for improvement.

- Listen and keep adapting to your customers feedback to get as close to perfection as possible.

11

COMPANY CULTURE

> An organization's ability to learn, and translate
> that learning into action rapidly, is the
> ultimate competitive advantage.
>
> —Jack Welch

If you grow a company from 5 to 500 employees in a short time like we did, there's going to be some chaos, and you can't avoid it. You'll most likely be frustrated in some situations and realize it's a part of the process. No one builds a company at scale without the chaos that happens along the way—the structure and stability of a business comes with time. While growth pains and typical business chaos is happening, don't get frustrated, embrace it instead. You may fire people and then hire another that leaves you for reasons you cannot explain. I think that's normal if you're growing fast. Just enjoy the ride and don't get caught in desperation during those times. You can work on the structure and stability over time.

As the business grows, in one moment everything seems under your control and then the next moment everything seems out of control. Most entrepreneurs will tell you this if they are being honest. You eventually need people to help monitor the day-to-day business operations for you. It's easier to manage 10 employees by yourself and have everyone do exactly how you want things done. As you grow, you need to delegate a lot of things, and it can be very uncomfortable. There will be employees who cannot meet your standard. There will be others who won't deliver the results you expected. Allow people to make mistakes. Even if you don't like it, people will make mistakes. Our role is to lead them; just like in sports, we act as the coach. The coach is always on the sidelines: watching the big picture. In the World Cup, sometimes the coach freaks out, but the coach never charges onto the field and kicks the ball, right? Running a business is quite analogous: you may have a knee-jerk reaction to freak out, but you never take over the work yourself. You help them. You coach them. But, let them make their own errors, and then you can just talk to them afterward. This takes discipline, and it's not easy. I think this has been one of the biggest challenges and learning experiences that we have gone through. When we started, we were much more emotional and quicker to react, and as we grew and learned and reflected, we always improved on this. Anyone new to business leadership, or who may not be a natural leader, may find this challenging. Embrace it, and as your company grows, your character and leadership will grow as well. If you master this, you'll become successful. If not, you'll find yourself limited by time-consuming operational tasks, not working to grow the business.

MISSION AND OFFICE CULTURE

Our company mission statement was just created in 2018: "Make a positive impact for a more sustainable Mexico." If you want an attractive workplace for employees, you must have a clear mission and plan. The process of writing down the plan ensures your business's future is defined. Ask yourself these questions: What is my motivation? What am I doing? What am I doing with this company? Write down all your answers and consider the group of people who work with you. Involve the people inside your company with developing this purpose and mission. Your mission and purpose need to be at the forefront of the conversation; you must always be forward thinking. Many of largest companies on the public market started with a clear purpose and mission. The mission may evolve and change over time, and that is okay.

I think if your mission doesn't involve something positive in the world, people may drift off and do something else. We both have had a green-conscious and sustainability focus from our early days. Our good practices from the beginning get people excited to join our company and its mission. This ensures a common mindset among employees; they feel like they are making a difference, and they are. We created a business plan that inspires, and our values connect us not only with a like-minded workforce but also with clients who want to collaborate and share the same values. In the office, we connect with our coworkers to get their feedback and insight into what matters to them.

Every month, we allow the different departments to give feedback on leadership and culture. We do this usually in a unanimous survey, and it has been very beneficial. If they are happy, we ask them what else we can do as a company to do better. Your employees will eventually be engaging with your clients directly, so they can offer some great insights into your company as you grow. We ask clients how we can get better. We want to know if they have everything they need, and what else we can do to make our service better. Part of our culture is to have a company meeting every two weeks where we all come together under one roof. We have a lot of meetings in the area, but not always together. So, every two weeks, we do an event where we talk about all the challenges as a company, as well as meet and present the new collaborators. We celebrate the wins and milestones we have reached together.

We're a very dynamic company with a lot of different products, so meetings and teams can be complex. We think what is truly important is that we share a common mission. The company must have a purpose-driven mission where the team can find alignment with its own identity and values. If people are working for the same goal, the company culture is like a beautiful orchestra working together. Of course, we have an amazing 3-level office that we built as well in Central Park. When we designed it, we had less than 10 people working for us, but we already planned the company's expansion and growth. After 1 year in the office we basically outgrew it and it was getting very challenging to fit everyone. It was designed by one of the top architects in our area, who is on our team. The office lets in lots of natural light, and it's comfortable for our team. It was inspired by the sustainable offices used by Google. It fits for us because we're a design-driven company, and our mission is to focus on sustainability. For example, we have transparent solar panels on the façade and a drinking water system that makes water out of the air. Also, it's very green inside. We also have a cool co-working area for our people to meet and gather, as well as rooftop games, such as ping pong and foosball, to take breaks and keep our minds fresh. We have realized that employees really appreciate a comfortable working space. As you can see, each and every detail makes the difference. This affects our external clients as well as our own talent.

BEING A DIFFERENTIATOR

When we visit other areas of Mexico, we see many development projects. It's a very dynamic country compared to Europe. Most of these are land and real estate development, but the projects are rarely sustainable. We saw the potential for integrating sustainable technology here, and then started using it within our company. Many construction workers are working on sustainable and green projects, and there's lots of work available right now. It's rare to find construction companies that use technology that is environmentally friendly and sustainable. That is how we're disruptive in this market: we aren't just sustainable as a company but also we're trying to make a positive environmental impact on the world by influencing the market to follow our lead in sustainability.

Leaving a positive environmental impact is not only a company mission but part of every operational practice. We've proven that it's possible to develop sustainable products that are cool. For example, we have a Smart Flower, a large solar panel structure that resembles a flower, in front of our main office in Tulum—people see it as a sculpture, a work of art. We have products that are attractive and, frankly, better than anything else in the market. Our infrastructures are safe, and we have a water treatment plant on several properties to provide clean drinking water and reduce energy costs. We strive to be the best that we can at green-conscious and sustainable real estate development. We produce more renewable energy than anyone else in the entire state. This is just a byproduct of our mission.

We're both passionate about the positive impact our product and business practices can have on the environment around the world. We get excited about creating energy from renewable sources, the technology that helps reduce energy consumption, building networks of charging stations for electric cars, and pioneering zero emission passenger drones. We have free conferences and learning seminars at our Los Amigos Academy where the locals can get free education, and we hope to take this model into other markets. We started with only our own employees sharing a talent or skill with other employees in the company, and then opened it up to the public to also speak and attend the events. We try to host 2 per month at our Los Amigos Cine project, where we built a private movie theater in the jungle. Yes, a private dinner-theater in the jungle!

These are areas that our guests and investors get excited about as well. Our company is an organization of people who share the same goal and impact. We're all connected through this!

SUSTAINABILITY

Before we started the company, Los Amigos, Nico worked within the renewable energy industry. He was leading the installation of solar panels into three different solar plants in Germany. Then the law was enacted connecting renewable energy to the utility companies in Germany. The idea is that the solar plant connects to the grid and then to consumers. Instead of paying for electricity, energy comes from a source that never stops: the sun.

We now produce and use more solar power than any other company in our region, and the sun will never send us a bill. The energy is free, and then we can store any excess energy for additional months. In Mexico you still can't get paid if you have extra solar energy, so the goal is to have enough solar technology to try and get grid consumption as low as possible. That's our business model: everyone wins. There's a demand for more energy, and solar power can easily be captured by a solar panel.

Mexico has great potential to generate most of its energy using renewable methods. In the Pacific, solar parks could be built on the abundant rooftop spaces. With this unique potential for solar energy, we often wonder why no one else is doing anything about it. So, in our first project, we integrated solar power, and we became the first residence to have this type of technology to power our properties.

All the energy needed to operate renewable technology is zero emission. The houses we built are powered by solar, and we integrated renewable energy technology in every aspect of our business. Now, we have transparent solar panels, the Smart Flower, which is one of the most advanced solar-powered systems in the world. As well we just installed one of the most high-tech solar wind turbines from England—the first installed in Latin America. This is on one of our newest projects called Central Park Lagunas. We aim to show people that everything is possible when striving to make a project sustainable.

We started Los Amigos with sustainability in mind. Choosing sustainability should be fundamental to every business, and it's not easy. We see protests around the world about wanting a change in the youth. But the change must be for how most people live, not just in a self-sustainable lifestyle. We strongly believe that we're all responsible for the well-being of our planet. We all need to learn and change, and our business furthers the conversation about businesses doing their part by implementing sustainable models.

At first, we didn't consider cultivating a certain reputation, because if you're a small company, the only thing your focused on is obtaining new clients. You're focused on client feedback because that's the best way to improve your business. When we were starting out, we personally checked in thousands of our customers. We provided 24-hour service and catered to all their needs. I really mean everything: from cleaning their toilets to refilling their water to airport transportation. Serving the guests well and giving them a great experience motivates them to tell other people about the company's mission and their great experience with the company. They'll likely write a positive review, and this will create a good reputation for your business over time. This is your brand. No need to spend a lot of money on branding; their feedback forms your company's brand.

We have no formal experience in hospitality, but we focused on giving our customers a great experience. We must make sure they get the best service. Sometimes, we encourage possible negative feedback so that we can improve the quality of our service. For example, if one of our guests makes a comment about low water pressure in the shower, we keep that in mind, and we go to work on it right away. One time a guest suggested having a bigger refrigerator: we made a serious note about it and considered it in the future. It's always best to listen to customers because they will tell you where and how you can do better.

We were invited to an event recently where someone asked us, "You have 19 units as an Airbnb Superhost and thousands of guests, how do you manage everything?" Our answer: "Keep asking for guest feedback." That's the best thing about getting customer feedback. You can improve on things before they become a problem. As we grew, we got further and further from direct contact with our guests. We ensure as the company grows that we always listen to and act on customer feedback.

We're thankful to have a good system and great people. Everything is now organized as a system, and the company runs near perfect. Still, there will always be problems that arise. For example, when a guest complains about slow internet, or the television doesn't work, we have a system in place to handle this problem. Customer service with real estate clients and real estate guests are two different things. Real estate is all about trust because the relationship is often lengthy. When clients are happy with your service, they stay with you. If you do a great job, people stick with you because no one wants to risk a bad vacation.

* * *

TIPS

- Learn to become a great leader, not a great manager.

- If you don't have a mission and a vision, create one now!

- A comfortable workspace is one of the most important things for your team.

- To be a sustainable business you must apply the 3 Ps: people, planet, and profit.

12

THE CORE BUSINESS

Sometimes when you innovate, you make
mistakes. It is best to admit them quickly and
get on with improving your other innovations.

—Steve Jobs

As we grew, it became apparent to us that we
needed to stay focused on the core of the business,
and not let side projects distract us. In the
beginning, we were taking on every opportunity.
When we started having success in our original
real estate development model, it seemed like new
opportunities, ideas, and projects were coming up
every month. As we scaled up and grew at a fast
pace, we wanted to stay in control of the timelines
and quality of each part of our project. When we
started offering more amenities, such as the spa,
gym, and restaurants, we knew we could manage

it because we had the client flow to support the new growth. We initially thought we could grow this way with hard work alone. We were experts on rental management at this stage. We thought all these additional operations we kept offering would be simple enough to run ourselves.

As we progressed, and we put each of these operations in motion while managing around 100 units at the time, we quickly realized that it was too much to handle. There were so many employees already, and managing all these new divisions spread the two of us entirely too thin. About 90 percent of our income came from real estate sales, and 10 percent from operations and management of the properties; however, we spent 90 percent of our time on operational management and only 10 percent on real estate development. Spending the majority of time on the day-to-day operations resulted in the lowest profit return for our time. While we loved to manage the operations, and we were good at it, we decided to focus on the core of the business, where most of the profits were. Real business profits came from real estate growth.

Many people make the same mistake we did. We wanted to have our hands in many things and do everything on our own. We also made plans to start a rental car company. We bought several vehicles because we had a lot of guests who wanted to rent vehicles during their stay at our properties. Then we realized that setting up these operations and adding more services was time-consuming and divided our focus. We wanted to start a tour company because we always had guests asking about tours. We wanted to do airport transportation with vans. We could see these short-term opportunities for cash flow, but our long-term vision and health was suffering. Things never got easier. This is an ongoing challenge for us, because we have always operated years ahead of our actual capacity and our growth. We're always stretching and testing our limits. We had to do it that way because Tulum's growth was fast paced. We felt like we were at a race against the growth of other competition. That's why we rarely slow down. We decided to find an operator for our company that could implement the operations we were running. At first, we thought that we could make more money if we did it ourselves, but we realized it wasn't worth it. By focusing on our core, we were able to scale and grow faster than ever.

When starting a new business, the moment it becomes viable, get external companies or operators in each of the other areas that is not your main focus. Always stay steady and focus on the core of the business. We'd have benefited from that advice early on. To this day, we're still transitioning to this kind of mentality, and so our company is growing.

DOWNSIZING

In such a small town it can be difficult to find employees, especially experienced professional employees. Also, because we're located in an amazing jungle environment, with a beach close by, the cost of living is relatively expensive, so it can be difficult finding workers, or convincing workers to come here, for standard rates of pay. People typically only visit Tulum for vacation—so, for example, we went through about five human resource professionals to find the right long-term fit for our company.

With the rapid growth of the company and the vision of our future developments, it was a challenge finding employees capable of running everything smoothly. We considered slowly downsizing the operation by looking for operating partners to work with us as a third party or a silent partner.

When we finished our second master project, Panoramic, with 84 units, our plan was to manage it all for the owners. But after our first project, we realized that even though we felt we could do the best job at managing, the energy that this new project would require would inhibit the company's overall growth. We took on and completed more big projects once we learned to loosen up our control over the management side of our business.

We hired a hotel operator to operate the apartments. That was one of the best first decisions we made about whether to expand the operational side. Most people would say not to give away a great business, but it's not great business if it reduces focus on the more lucrative business model. So, our payroll for operations may decrease, but it does not necessarily mean that the operations employees will be on the street. Hiring ten people a week is not necessary anymore. We're not laying off people, but slowly as employee turnover happens, we restructure the positions. Most operations staff that work in these positions will probably work for the new management company.

INVESTORS

As our land development and vacation–rental service grew more and more successful, people began noticing. Different investors, companies, and landowners are interested in Tulum now. Now we're one of the largest companies in the market. Over the years many people have come to us to offer capital investments or to try to sell their property to us. At this point, we have slowed down on buying land. We no longer need to invest our own capital. Our brand and knowledge have become our biggest asset.

We've started a project for an investor who is unsure about how to develop his land. It's a lot of work and most people don't have the time, energy, or knowledge for it. Since a lot of people want us to develop their land for them, the model has evolved into the investor providing us their land, while we lead the development project and have a profit share agreement. We like that model because we're not using our own capital. And the project is built and funded on preconstruction sales. The buyers make a down payment for their unit, and that down payment finances the majority of the construction.

This business model allows us to solely focus on designing, building, and selling properties. This is where we really excel. We're not looking for land anymore and then searching for the capital to fund it. We're partnering with bigger and bigger companies now. We're now partnered with Inmobilia; the partnership began on our latest project called 101 Park. The project is in a new area of Tulum near the beach and will contain 181 units on around 2 hectares (approximately 5 acres). Inmobilia is one of the biggest developers in the southeast region as well and one of the only developers in the region on the public stock market. This has become a way for us to expand faster.

The deals are unique to each investor. Our main focus is to do a project that has a lot of sustainable technology and, of course, gives a positive return on investment, for both the company and for the partner. Everybody agrees with the terms up front, and everyone wins. We're always sure to be very transparent and clear about the terms to protect everyone involved. The proportion of the profits varies depending on the type of project. Either way, the landowners get more money with a properly built development than they would have gotten if the investor had sold the land. There is a longer delay profiting from the land, but the deal always ends up better for them long-term.

Our company has a great track record; the Los Amigos brand is global and now has vast experience, which is why we're able to land these deals. If you are just starting, be patient and work on your first deal. It doesn't matter that you're not starting with a million-dollar project. Do things right. Develop a positive track record over time and put in the sweat. The more significant deals will come to you over time if you focus on your core business and do it well.

* * *

TIPS

- Look at what's the core of your business and focus on this right away.

- Don't bite off more than you can chew.

- Find creative deals with land investors, and you provide the work and know-how, not the capital.

- Look for partners to help you in areas that are important but not your main focus so that you can expand faster and put more energy into your core.

13

THE FUTURE

If you get up in the morning and think the
future is going to be better, it's a bright day.

—**Elon Musk**

Our mission is to create a positive impact by running
a green-conscious, sustainable, environmentally
friendly company. The evolution of a company is
similar to the growth of an athlete: you first start
in your own small town; if you play well, you move
up to the state level; then the national league; and
then the world championship!

Sustainability and real estate development in
Mexico are exciting. As much as possible, we'd like
to establish a strong foundation of sustainability;
we're careful not to outgrow our values.

As we enter new markets around the world, we want to know every street, every corner, and every piece of land so that we know how to market there. This is what we did in Tulum for the first few years. Aside from that, we're looking for trustworthy partners in each new market. This is very crucial as you grow, and we already have a lot of people contacting us for partnerships around Mexico and the world. We value the strengths of other companies and expert insight, and we plan to build on this going forward into the future. This has formed the principles of Los Amigos today. Hopefully, our initiatives will yield further global market expansions in the next few years.

Dubai and China are also areas we're both very interested in investing and developing. We see the high potential to grow globally and would like to expand the Los Amigos brand internationally. That's our next big move. But most importantly, in each new region, we will start on a small scale and expand from there—first, a small development and have each development become larger than the next. The same successful model we employed in Tulum.

Risks will always be there. Sure, we have a little more capital to work with now, but we still need to make smart choices, and we're up to taking on new challenges. We also want to adapt the company's image as we grow our global Los Amigos brand. The needs and potential opportunities with our current clients and investors carry much weight in our decision-making. Similar to our previous projects, we will find an untapped piece of land, develop a property, and use our experience and wisdom to duplicate our success in new markets. Sure, we may make mistakes in a new market, but that comes with the territory of being an entrepreneur.

TIPS TO INSPIRE YOUNG ENTREPRENEURS

After talking to countless entrepreneurs and CEOs over the years, the single commonality is that every small project starts with a big vision. Think global and start local.

Today, new land developers can get started and get backed by a larger company. We have considered partnering with no-name developers in another country where they have access to the local resources of that country. We'd provide the brand name and our vision and work out a percentage deal. That's how we can grow internationally and not have to be there physically.

Many developers already do this. As a growing entrepreneur, seek out developers you can partner with and share your vision with them. You would be amazed at the opportunities that arise when you start with a big vision for your company and are open to partnerships. Instead of looking at the financial aspects of a partnership first, share with them potential partners, your commitment, and your big vision. Investing globally over the next few years will be a game changer. Be sure to learn about how your market works on a global scale. By being aware of the market status, you'll notice market trends, and your keen market insights and knowledge will attract new investors.

It is essential that you understand the larger financial markets and gain a basic understanding of public markets as you grow. Remember to start local, think global. Some developers are still using the old school business strategies of getting a massive loan and putting all their eggs in one basket when a market is untested with a smaller project first. Smaller initial investments will inform the viability of your business model.

INNOVATIVE TECHNOLOGIES CREATE INTEREST

We have also utilized technology and disruptive innovations to attract new investors. One of our latest innovations to incorporate new technology is the passenger drone, which is a personal air vehicle. Over fifty companies are actively developing and improving the technology of passenger drones. The passenger drones have one or two seats, with an interior similar to a car. The only company in the world that is really at the stage of flying passenger drones is a company out of China called Ehang. They have filed paperwork with the US Securities and Exchange Commission with 100 million shares on the Nasdaq stock market. (Nico actually represented Los Amigos at the New York Stock Exchange when the stock went public and rang the bell with Ehang, which was cool!) We're very excited about the opportunities created by passenger drones. There is always a problem with traffic, and the markets of real estate and transportation are connected.

People now buy homes further away from their workplace, resulting in more and more traffic. We're currently all stuck in one dimension with our current transportation system: roads and highways.

Between the ground and 1,000 meters into the air, there is no traffic—only a few birds watching us all stuck in traffic, laughing. We need to move our transportation schema into three-dimensional space, and the passenger drones are a perfect solution. We're so sure about this that we have already ordered our first autonomous, zero-emission drone, and we will be one of the first companies in the world to utilize this passenger drone. This human transport drone is extremely safe. It operates fully electric, and with 16 propellers. It doesn't require a pilot as its fully autonomous. A common helicopter is very dangerous because it runs on a combustion engine and has only one propeller. Farmers can use drones for their crops, hospitals to transport organs, and companies for a tourism attraction. We believe this will revolutionize transportation, and we're going to be pioneers of this new technology. It will be arriving to Tulum in the Spring of 2020, so next time you visit us, we hope that you can fly in it!

Making your vision known to the world will turn it into a reality since your investment opportunities will be compelling to investors. It's best to understand what model or strategy you use because each market will have its own unique need. The thing is, we see people talking about sustainable development, but we don't see much action. In order to win clients and investors, you need to make sure that you present your vision in a positive and exciting way. You have to color a vision that speaks to their deep human needs. Let them see your vision first, followed by presenting the numbers. Once all these factors are combined, you'll end up with the investment that you need to fund your project. If not, tell your vision and mission to someone else. Someone will catch your vision and want to see it come to reality.

THE MOON PROJECT

We don't acknowledge that the sky's the limit. We have a grander vision where the sky has no limits. We plan to have flying drones very soon in Tulum, but beyond that, we have developed a moon project. Seriously, we have renders, architectural plans, and plenty of research by our design team.

Commercial space travel is on the horizon of possibility. Although we don't have a rocket to get to the moon, there are companies right now who are marketing this idea internationally. They're searching for people willing to go to the moon for a reasonable price.

We're researching how we can reduce the market costs and come up with an infrastructure starting in Tulum. Imagine being able to reserve a round-trip travel ticket to the moon online as easily as getting an airplane ticket from New York to Los Angeles. Pretty exciting, right? The more we think about it, providing people with an affordable experience to the moon is unlike anything else! You can just imagine how life-changing it would be to see the Earth from the moon—being able to experience how it feels to be there, how it feels traveling through space. This project needs a sustainability focus and development. We have limited resources, but we know that with the right support and alignment of our vision with investors, the moon project will be possible. To this day everything that we have wanted to achieve we have. Although this will be the biggest feat yet, it's only a matter of years until this will happen too.

ENTERING THE PUBLIC MARKET

Most entrepreneurs are gifted with the ability to create and to build something from nothing. All business types have something unique to offer. If you are an entrepreneur and you see that your business income trends the same rate year after year, then something is wrong. You have to take your time to study which aspects need to be addressed. You were meant for growth and abundance.

Once you create some momentum, make each project larger than the last, and always keep building on your momentum. Your projects will eventually become very attractive to investors, and they will be making you offers. Experts naturally would like to invest in your business once they see momentum. So, the next step to consider once you begin to grow on a larger scale is to bring your company to the public market. The public then has an opportunity to invest in your business and be a part of its growth. Creating a bigger company impact can be possible through the public market because more people are financially interested in your vision and company.

Sustainability is another thing to consider. You may want to find something that brings personal interest to consumers. Investors want to invest in a mission and cause they believe in. Customers also want to buy products from companies with a cause or mission. People who believe in taking care of the environment are attracted to sustainable and environmentally conscious companies. If the company's vision is clear and attractive to them, people will be interested in your vision.

When running a company in Mexico, or any other country for that matter, you have to think globally if you wish to someday offer your company in the public market. There's only a small percentage of companies that make it to the public market. A smaller percentage of those companies come from Mexico because most of them don't keep accountable records and accounting. Your local government may not regulate your company and have a strict auditing process like the Internal Revenue Service in the United States. However, it's vitally important in the public market. We see this as a considerable advantage for us. Everything we do is clean and above board regarding our accounting. We have always tried to run our businesses from the beginning to meet the bookkeeping standards in the US, although challenging. This way, if we decide to take a company public, we already have everything in order. There really is massive potential for any growing company if you get the business numbers right. It might not happen this month or next year, but most likely, in the next 4–5 years you can position yourself for a great lifestyle and a thriving business. Nothing worthwhile happens overnight. Real, sustainable growth is there for you, and it's possible. We did it, and you can do it too if you work hard, treat your staff right, and put your customer's interests first to give them a positive and unforgettable experience from your products or services.

Maybe you'll meet us one day, in a spacious lunar lounge, and you can tell us about your journey to the moon!

* * *

TIPS

- Dominate your market locally first, then look national, then international. Start local, think global!

- Look for investors and partners to expand with. Don't focus on just the money but think long term.

- Anything you put your mind to is possible; don't give up or let the people get you down.

Is the sky the limit? Or is it the moon?!

ABOUT THE AUTHORS

MARC LEVY

Marc Levy grew up in Scottsdale, Arizona. From a young age, Marc always had an entrepreneurial spirit— at ten years old he was selling snacks in a red wagon at the local baseball games. Marc completed his Bachelor of Science in construction at Arizona State University. He's worked in the construction industry as a project engineer and invested in real estate. Marc is LEED (Leadership in Energy and Environmental Design) accredited and PMP (Project Management Professional) certified. Marc leads Los Amigos operations team and makes sure that all decisions, present and future, are aligned with the vision of the company. Marc is Co-Founder and COO.

NICO WILMES

Nico Wilmes, entrepreneur and former Mr. Millennium, hails from Germany, where he worked in the cardboard packaging business. The renewable energy industry was his passion. He revolutionized the use of renewable energy, especially solar power, on rental vacation properties in Mexico. Nico saw the potential in Tulum, Mexico, way before most people. His vision, risk taking, and constant forward-thinking has helped Los Amigos to grow at an exponential pace. Nico goes on tour speaking about "Mexico Chingón" and inspires people to go for their dreams. Nico is Co-Founder and CEO.

Made in the USA
Monee, IL
16 April 2022